TEAM Together Starter

Activity Book

T0345722

Contents

1 🖊 **Look, trace and draw.**

1 ✏️ **Look and colour.**

 1   2   3   4   5   6

 # Friends and family

1 **Listen. Look and match.**

1

2

a

b

2 **Listen, find and stick.**

a
b
c
d

Language practice

1 🎧 1.8 ✏️ **Listen and circle.**

1   a   b

2   a   b

2 💥 **Draw and share.**

1 🎧 1.10 ✏️ **Listen. Look and number.**

2 ✏️ **Look and colour.**

Values ✔️ **Be helpful**

Language practice

1 (1.16) **Listen, find and stick.**

a  b  c  d

2 (1.17) 🖍 **Listen and tick (✔).**

1 a  b

2 a  b

1 🖊 **Look and colour. B** ✳ **b** ✳ **.**

rBubTmbwB

2 🖊 **Look and connect Bb.**

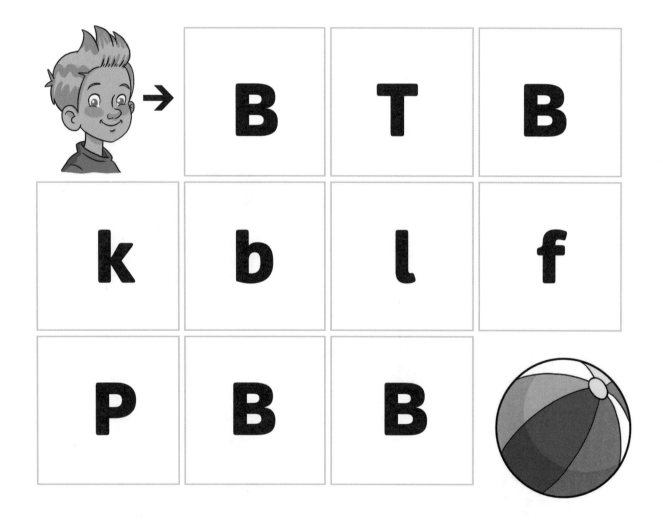

1 🖍 **Look and colour. D ✸ d ✸ .**

DpdDuefdc

2 🖍 **Look and connect Dd.**

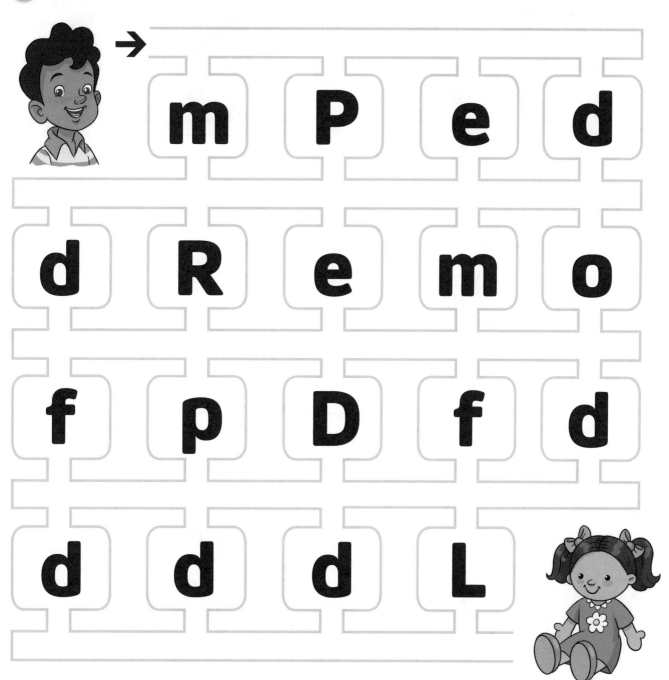

1 🎧 (1.22) ✏️ **Listen and tick (✓).**

1

a    b   ☐

2

a   b   ☐

3

a   b   ☐

4

a   b   ☐

2 🎧 (1.23) ✏️ **Listen and colour.**

1 🎧 1.26 ✏️ **Listen and number.**

2 🎧 1.27 ✏️ **Listen and match.**

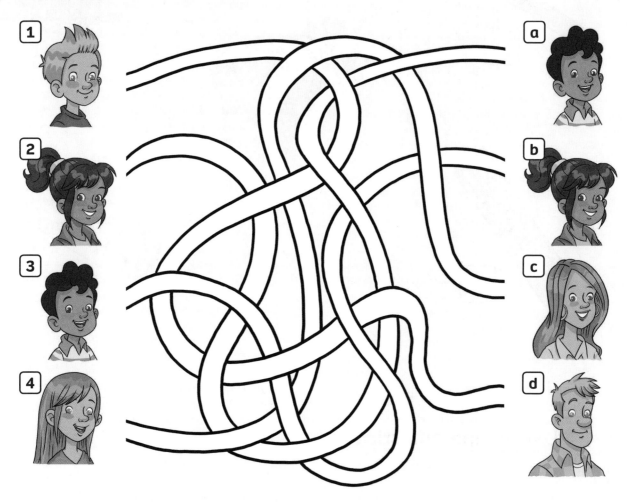

3 ✏️ **Look and colour for Unit 1.**

 **My school bag**

1 (2.3) 🖊️ **Listen. Look and tick (✔).**

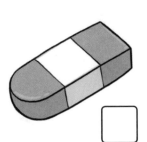

2 (2.4) 🎧 **Listen, find and stick.**

a	b	c	d

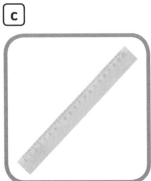

Language practice

1 **Listen and match.**

   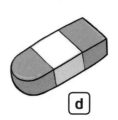

2 **Draw and share.**

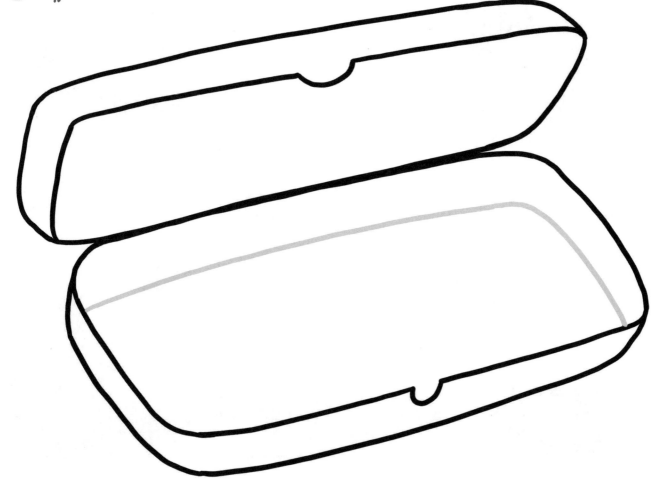

1 🎧 2.10 ✏️ **Listen. Look and number.**

2 ✏️ **Look and colour.**

Values ✓ Look after your things

1 🎧 2.16 **Listen, find and stick.**

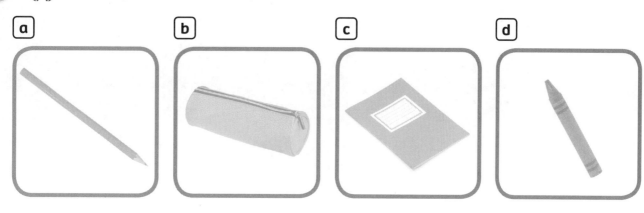

| a | b | c | d |

2 🎧 2.17 ✏️ **Listen and tick (✔).**

1 a   b

2 a   b

3 a   b

1 🖍 **Look and colour. P** ✹ **p** ✹ **.**

LpPejoPlpe

2 🖍 **Look and connect Pp.**

p	P	F	b
f	C	p	w	D
d	m	P	P	p
q	F	j	U	

1 ✏️ **Look and colour. R ✴ r ✴.**

remRrkwRx

2 ✏️ **Look and connect Rr.**

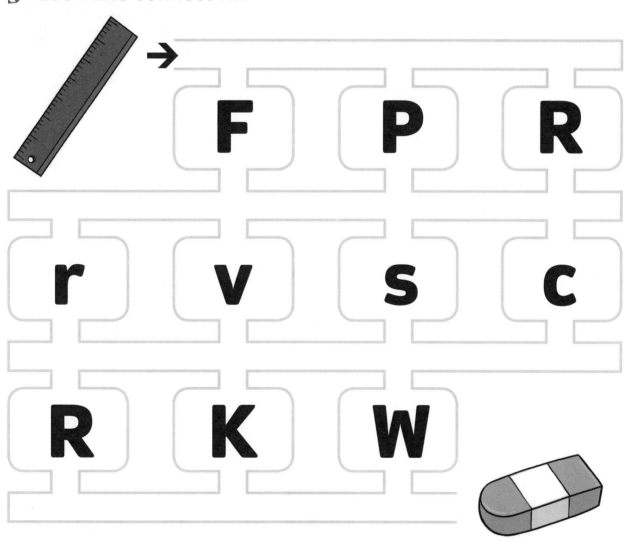

1  **2.22** 🖉 **Listen and circle.**

1

a   b

2

a   b

3

a   b

4

a   b

2 **2.23** 🖉 **Listen, cross (✗) and play!**

1 🎧 2.26 ✏️ **Listen and tick (✔) or cross (✘).**

a

b

c

d

2 🎧 2.27 ✏️ **Listen and draw.**

3 ✏️ **Look and colour for Unit 2.**

 Our classroom

1 (3.3) **Listen. Look and number.**

2 (3.4) **Listen, find and stick.**

a	b	c	d
	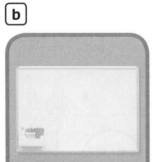		

1 🎧 3.8 ✏️ **Listen and circle.**

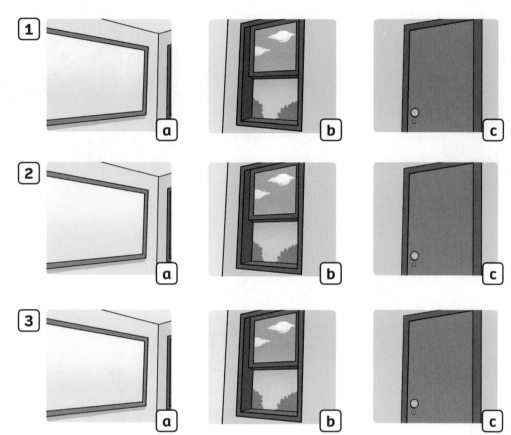

2 💥 **Draw and share.**

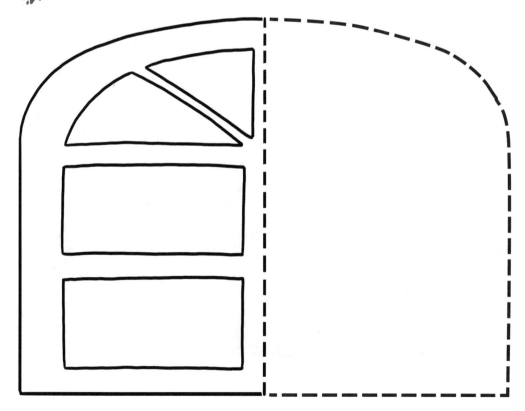

1 🎧 3.10 ✏️ **Listen. Look and number.**

a

b

c

d

e

2 ✏️ **Look and colour the circles.**

Values ✓ Be tidy

1

2

3

Language practice

1 🎧 3.16 **Listen, find and stick.**

a  b  c  d

2 🎧 3.17 ✏️ **Listen and match.**

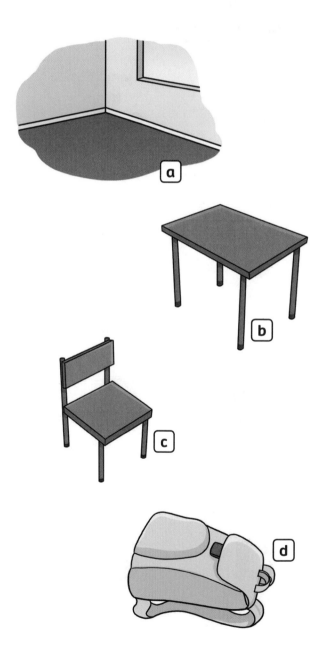

1 🖊 **Look and colour. C ✹ c ✹ .**

cyjCcqpCH

2 🖊 **Look and connect Cc.**

1 🖊 **Look and colour. W ✳ w ✳ .**

RwWpjewWF

2 🖊 **Look and connect Ww.**

w	**W**	**c**	**b**
G	**h**	**W**	**w**	**w**
R	**W**	**H**	**w**	**j**
P	**r**	**w**	**W**	**p**
g	**D**	**W**	**w**	

1 🎧 3.22 ✏️ Listen and tick (✔).

1

2
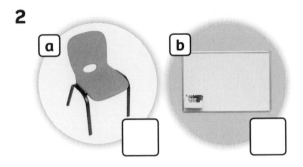

3

4

2 ✏️ Look and play!

1 3.25 🖊 **Listen and number.**

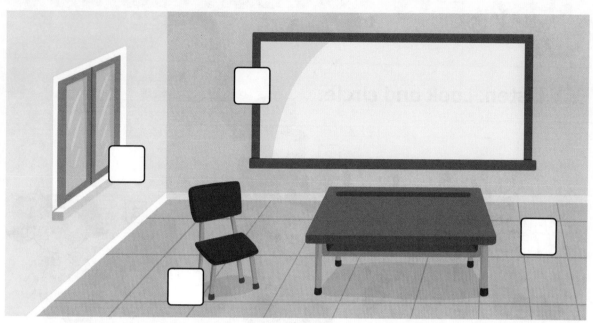

2 3.26 🖊 **Listen and draw.**

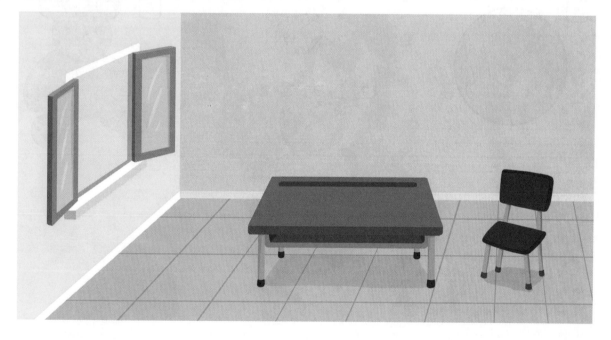

3 🖊 **Look and colour for Unit 3.**

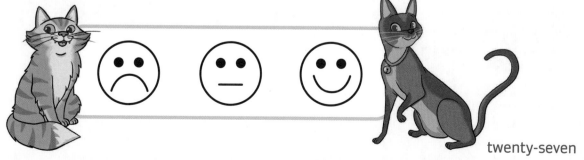

4 My favourite toy

1 **Listen. Look and circle.**

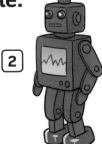

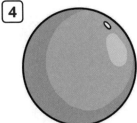

2 **Listen, find and stick.**

a	b	c	d

1 🎧 4.8 ✏️ **Listen and circle.**

1
a
b

2
a
b

3
a
b

4
a
b

2 💥 **Draw, colour and share.**

1 🎧 4.10 ✏️ **Listen. Look and number.**

a

b

c

d

e

2 ✏️ **Look and colour.**

Values ✔️ Share

1 **2**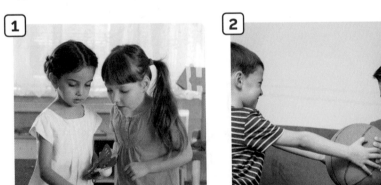

3

Language practice

1 (4.16) **Listen, find and stick.**

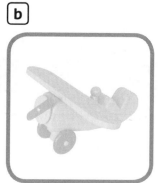
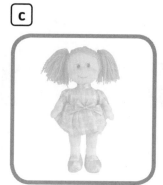
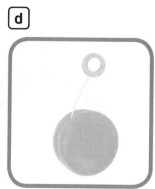

2 (4.17) 🖊 **Listen and match.**

1 🖊 Look and colour. T ✸ t ✸ .

TtsrmtkcT

2 🖊 Look and connect Tt.

m	r	T	t	T
t	b	l	t	A	T
t	H	t	T	E	t
t	t	T	M	b	t
f	L	R	e	p	

1 🖍 **Look and colour. Y ✳ y ✳ .**

mgYdyebyY

2 🖍 **Look and connect Yy.**

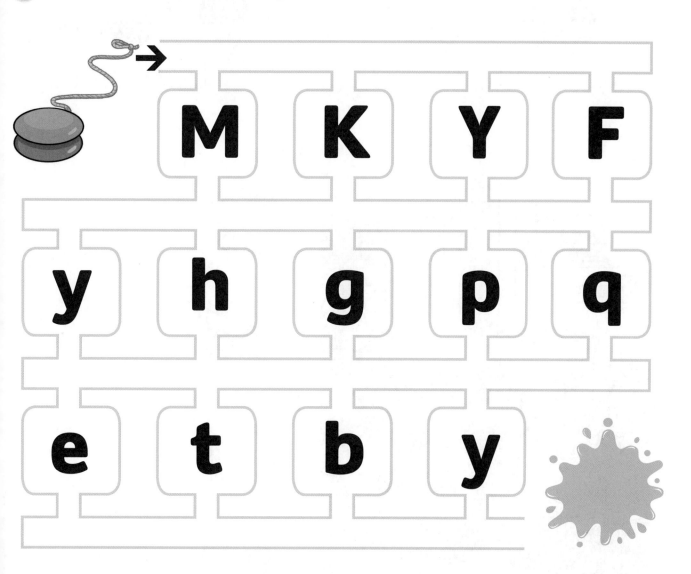

1 🎧 4.22 ✏️ **Listen and tick (✓).**

1
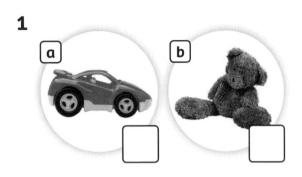

a b

2

a b

3
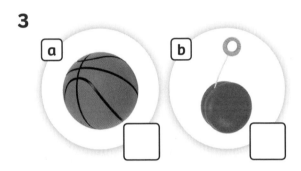

a b

4
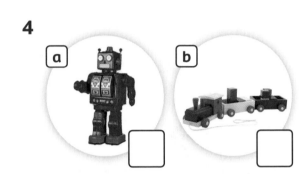

a b

2 ✏️ **Look, count and match. Then say.**

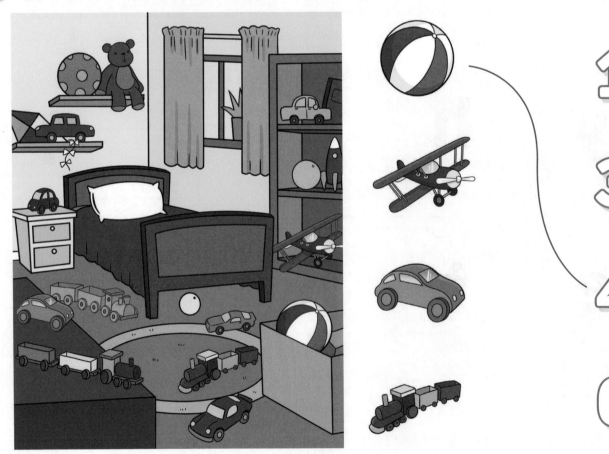

1

3

4

6

1 (4.25) 🖊 **Listen and number.**

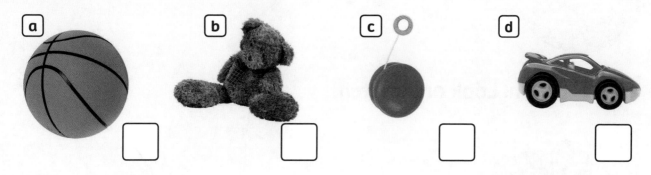

a   b   c   d

2 🖊 **Find, colour and say.**

3 🖊 **Look and colour for Unit 4.**

 # My body!

1 🎧 5.3 Listen. Look and match.

 **1**

 **2**

 **3**

 **4**

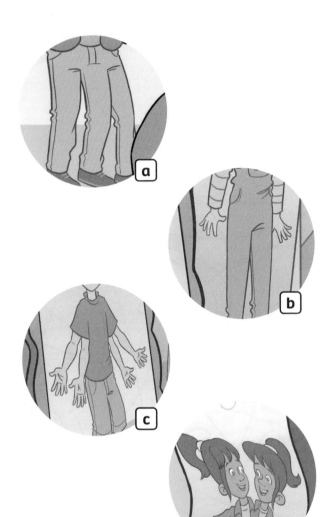

a

b

c

d

2 🎧 5.4 Listen, find and stick.

a

b

c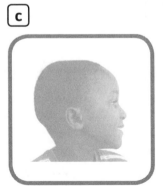

d

Language practice

1 🎧 5.8 ✏️ **Listen and tick (✔).**

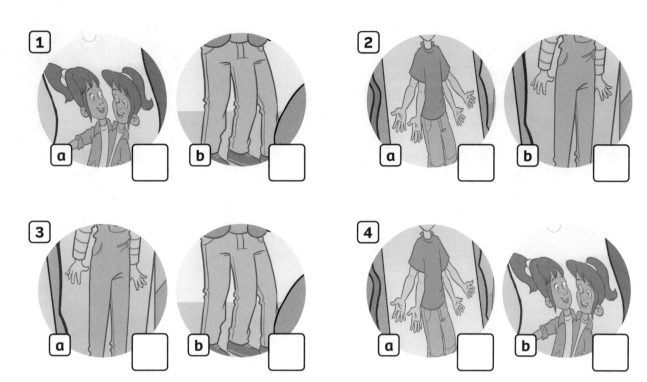

2 💥 **Draw and share.**

1  **Listen. Look and number.**

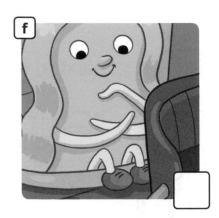

2  **Look and colour.**

 Values ✓ Be safe

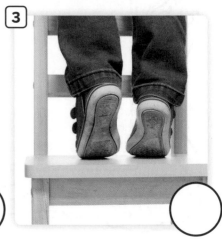

Language practice

1 🎧 5.16 **Listen, find and stick.**

a  **b**  **c** 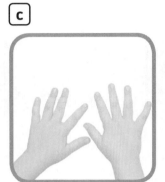 **d**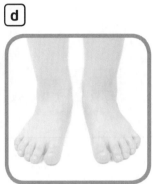

2 🎧 5.17 ✏ **Listen and number.**

1 🖊 **Look and colour. F ✳ f ✳ .**

f h d F f u F g t d

2 🖊 **Look and connect Ff.**

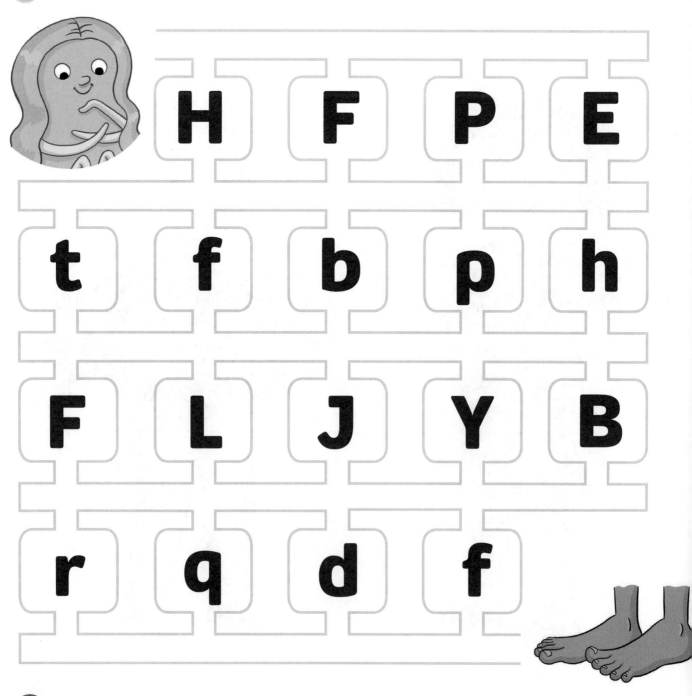

H	F	P	E
t	f	b	p	h
F	L	J	Y	B
r	q	d	f

1 ✏ **Look and colour. H ✹ h ✹ .**

h d v H K h t b H

2 ✏ **Look and connect Hh.**

H	h	h	h	E
e	o	p	f	H	r
h	H	h	h	H	D
h	L	H	h	h	H
h	H	h	B	b	

1  **Listen and circle.**

1

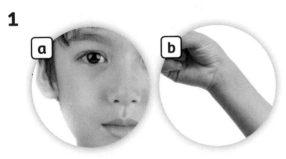

2

3

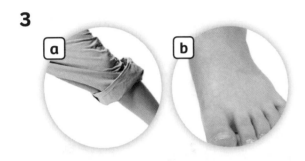

4

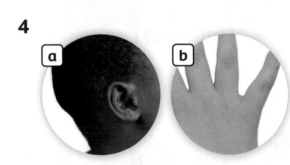

2 (5.23) **Listen and colour.**

1 🎧 5.26 ✏️ **Listen and number.**

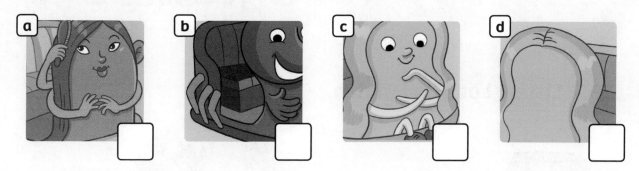

a   b   c   d

2 ✏️ **Colour and say.**

3 ✏️ **Look and colour for Unit 5.**

6 My blue jacket

1  **6.3 Listen. Look and match.**

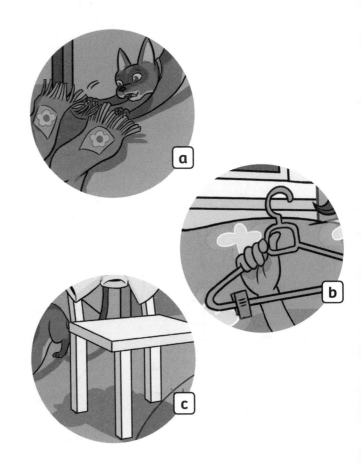

2 **6.4 Listen, find and stick.**

a	b	c	d
skirt	jumper	T-shirt	jacket

1  Listen and number.

a

b

c

d

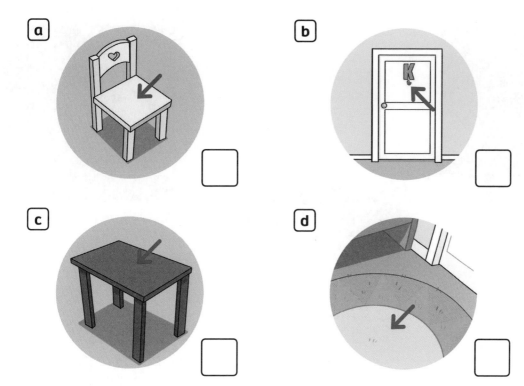

2 Draw and share.

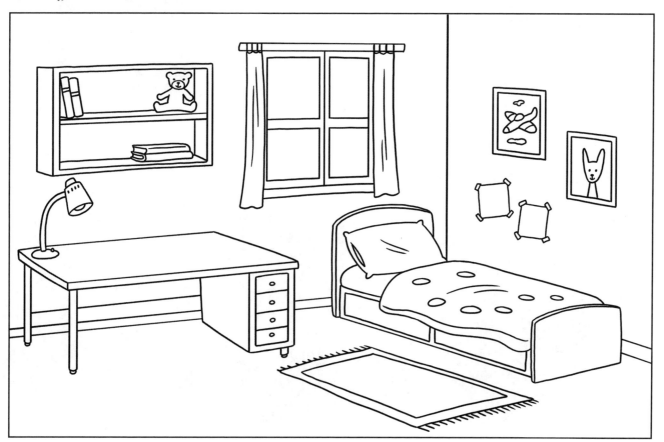

1 🎧 6.10 ✏️ **Listen. Look and number.**

a

b

c

d

e

2 ✏️ **Look and colour.**

Values ✓ **Be on time**

1

2

3

Language practice

1 (6.16) **Listen, find and stick.**

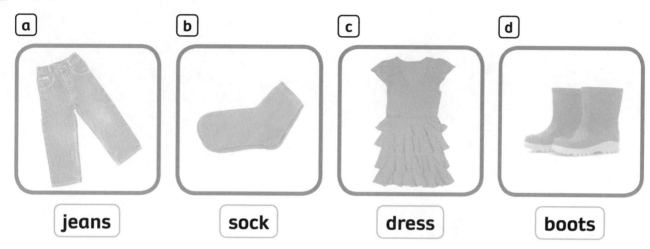

a	b	c	d
jeans	sock	dress	boots

2 (6.17) ✏ **Listen and draw.**

1 ✏️ **Look and colour. S** ✳️ **s** ✳️ **.**

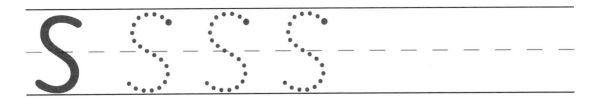

sncSrseSb

2 ✏️ **Look and trace.**

S S S S

S s s s

3 ✏️ **Look and trace.**

s socks

1   🖊 **Look and colour. J ✳ j ✳.**

jygJLjqbj

2   🖊 **Look and trace.**

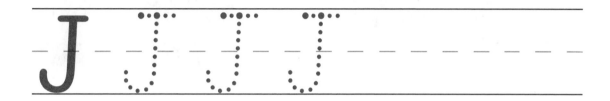

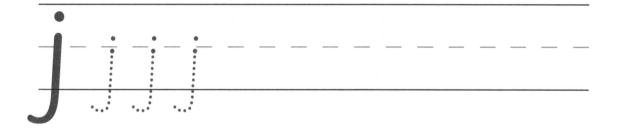

3   🖊 **Look and trace.**

 juice

1  **Listen and circle.**

1

a   b

2

a   b

3

a   b

4

a   b

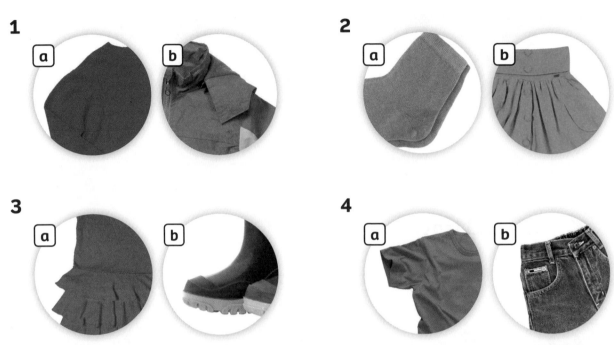

2 **Look, colour and say.**

1  Listen and match .

1  2  3  4

 a  b  c  d

2  Look and play.

Start →

   → Finish

3 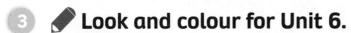 Look and colour for Unit 6.

They're tigers!

1 🎧 7.3 **Listen. Look and count.**

1 ☐ 2 ☐ 3 ☐ 4 ☐

2 🎧 6.4 **Listen, find and stick.**

a b c d

hippo zebra tiger monkey

1   **Listen and number.**

a

b

c

d

2  **Draw and share.**

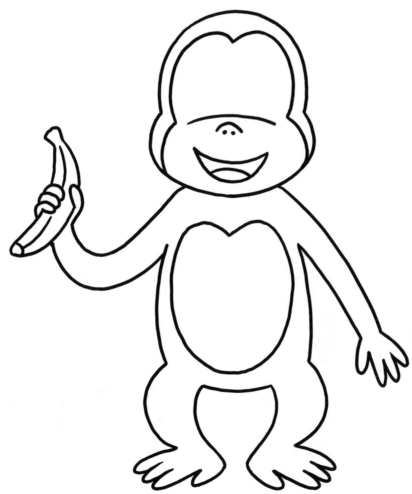

1  **Listen. Look and number.**

2  **Look and colour.**

 **Values** ✔ **Look after animals**

Language practice

1 🎧 7.16 **Listen, find and stick.**

a	b	c	d
snake	lizard	frog	spider

2 🎧 7.17 ✏️ **Listen and circle.**

1 🖍️ **Look and colour. M** ✳️ **m** ✳️ **.**

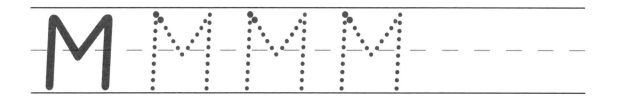

2 🖍️ **Look and trace.**

M M M M M ⎯ ⎯ ⎯

m m m m ⎯ ⎯ ⎯

3 🖍️ **Look and trace.**

m monkey

Letters and sounds Kk

1 🖊 **Look and colour. K ✳ k ✳ .**

f k h K H k t K S

2 🖊 **Look and trace.**

K K K K

k k k k

3 🖊 **Look and trace.**

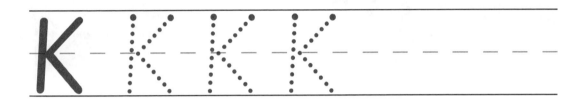

k kite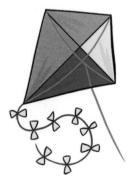

1  **Listen and tick.**

1

a b

2

a b

3

a b

4

a b

2 🖊️ **Look, match and say.**

1

2

3

4

a

b

c

d

1 🎧 7.25 ✏️ **Listen and number.**

a b c d

2 ✏️ **Find, say and tick (✔).**

3 ✏️ **Look and colour for Unit 7.**

☹️ 😐 🙂

8 I like cakes

1 8.3 **Listen. Look and circle.**

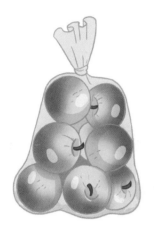

2 8.4 **Listen, find and stick.**

| a | b | c | d |

| lemonade | lemons | apples | cakes |

1   **Listen and tick (✔).**

1 a 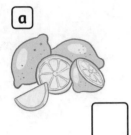 ☐   b 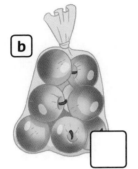 ☐   2 a  ☐   b ☐

3 a  ☐   b 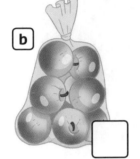 ☐   4 a 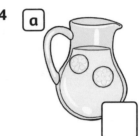 ☐   b 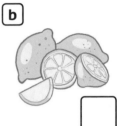 ☐

2 **Draw, colour and share.**

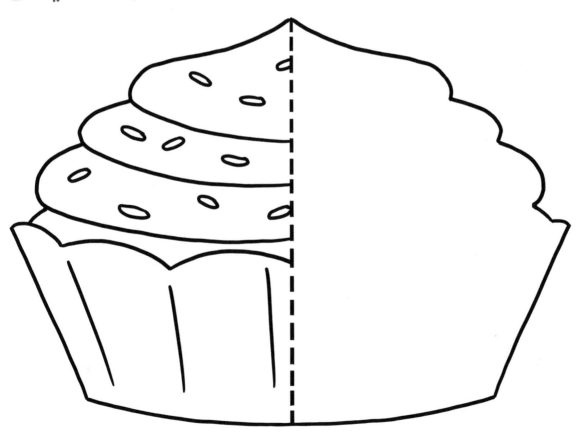

1 🎧 8.10 ✏️ **Listen. Look and number.**

a

b

c

d

e

2 ✏️ **Look and colour.**

Values ✔️ **Be polite**

1

2

3

Language practice

1 🎧 8.16 **Listen, find and stick.**

a	b	c	d

juice	carrots	grapes	sweets

2 🎧 8.17 ✏️ **Listen and draw.**

1 ✏️ **Look and colour. G ✳️ g ✳️.**

GdgPoguGy

2 ✏️ **Look and connect Gg.**

1 🖊 Look and colour. L  l ❋ .

LtilJLnlY

2 🖊 Look and trace.

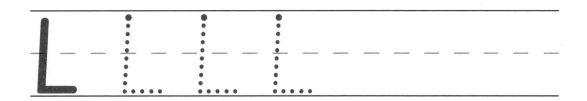

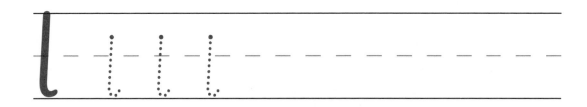

3 🖊 Look and trace.

l lemons lemons

1 (8.22) 🖊 **Listen and number.**

2 (8.23) 🖊 **Listen, cross (✗) and play!**

1 🎧 8.26 ✏️ **Listen and circle.**

2 ✏️ **Look and tick (✔). Then say.**

	☺	☹

3 ✏️ **Look and colour for Unit 8.**

1 ✏ **Look, trace and say.**

boy

brother

cat

dad

friend

girl

mum

sister

2 ✏ Look, number and say.

1 bag	**2** book	**3** crayon	**4** pen
5 pencil	**6** pencil case	**7** rubber	**8** ruler

3 **Look, match and say.**

chair

desk

door

floor

teacher

wall

whiteboard

window

4 🖊 **Look, tick (✔) and say.**

ball		
car		
doll		
plane		
robot		
teddy		
train		
yoyo		

5 ✎ **Look, number and say.**

arms ☐

body ☐

face ☐

feet ☐

hair ☐

hands ☐

head ☐

legs ☐

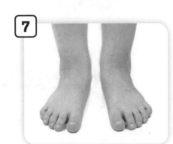

6 ✏️ **Trace and circle. Then say.**

boots			
dress			
jacket			
jeans			
jumper			
skirt			
socks			
T-shirt			

7 **Trace and match. Then say.**

frog

hippo

lizard

monkey

spider

snake

tiger

zebra

8 ✏ **Trace and circle. Then say.**

apples			
carrots			
cakes			
grapes			
juice			
lemonade			
lemons			
sweets			

Fun time

1 ✏️ **Count, write and trace.**

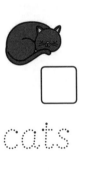

cats

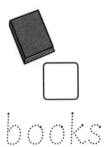

books

windows

balls

hands

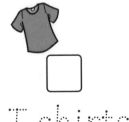

T-shirts

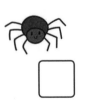

spiders

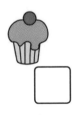

cakes

② ✏ **Look, colour and trace.**

1   2   3   4   5   6

seventy-seven **77**

Alphabet time

 A a

 B b

 C c

 D d

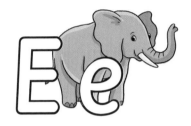 E e

 F f

 G g

 H h

 I i

 J j

 K k

 L l

 M m

 N n

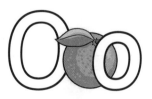 O o

 P p

 Q q

 R r

 S s

 T t

 U u

 V v

 W w

 X x

 Y y

 Z z

Pearson Education Limited
KAO TWO
KAO Park
Hockham Way
Harlow, Essex
CM17 9SR England
and Associated Companies throughout the world.

www.english.com/teamtogether

First published 2020
Sixth impression 2024
ISBN: 978-1-292-29249-6
Set in Daytona Pro Primary 16pt
Printed in Slovakia by Neografia

Image Credit(s):

123RF.com: 60, 75, acies 20, 26, 51, 70, Andrey Kiselev 36, 42, 72, aneva 66, Anton Starikov 47, 50, 51, 73, evaletova 44, 50, 51, 73, jirkaejc 39, 42, 72, Olga Popova 47, 50, 51, 73, pockygallery 15, 18, 69, raysay 38, Sirichai Asawalapsakul 60, 67, 75, Tamas Balogh 66, utima 66, wckiw 39, 42, 72; **Getty Images**: damircudic 38, Danger Dai 52, 58, 59, 74, Dave McKay 55, 58, 59, 74, goldenKB 4, 10, 68, hartcreations 36, 42, 72, in4mal 23, 26, 51, 70, JBryson 7, 10, 68, Johnny Greig 31, kupicoo 7, 7, 10, 10, 68, 68, monkeybusinessimages 4, 10, 30, 31, 68, Photographer's Choice 31, 34, 71, Ryan McVay 12, 18, 69, shalamov 54, skynesher 46, SolStock 20, 26, 70, Steven_Kriemadis 46, Wavebreakmedia 20, 26, 70, wdstock 63, 66, 67, 75; **Pearson Education Asia Ltd**: Joey Chan 44, 50, 51, 73; **Pearson Education Ltd**: Studio 8 4, 7, 10, 10, 31, 36, 42, 68, 68, 72; **Shutterstock.com**: AlesiaKan 22, Alfa Photostudio 22, Alla Ushakova 63, 66, 75, Anatoliy Sadovskiy 36, 42, 72, andras_csontos 62, Andresr 28, 34, 35, 71, Big Foot Productions 12, 18, 69, Billion Photos 14, Bjoern Wylezich 15, 18, 69, Chepurnova Oxana 47, 50, 51, 73, Christian Delbert 20, 26, 70, Dakalova Iuliia 31, 34, 71, Darren Baker 66, Deep OV 4, 10, 68, design56 12, 18, 69, Dieter H. 38, Eduardo Rivero 52, 58, 59, 74, Egor Rodynchenko 66, Evgeny Karandaev 63, 66, 67, 75, Harper 3D 55, 58, 59, 74, HK-PHOTOGRAPHY 66, Hurst Photo 46, Ivonne Wierink 31, 34, 71, JeniFoto 60, 66, 67, 75, Katerina-Kat 54, Lepas 63, 67, 75, Liga Alksne 28, 34, 35, 71, LightField Studios 14, Lightspruch 54, Lordn 6, Manuel Findeis 55, 58, 59, 74, Margo Harrison 23, 26, 51, 70, Marko Poplasen 23, 26, 70, MartinMaritz 52, 58, 59, 74, nfmlk 39, 42, 72, Nipaporn Panyacharoen 66, oksana2010 12, 18, 69, Olena Yakobchuk 6, Olena Zaskochenko 44, 50, 51, 73, Perutskyi Petro 39, 42, 72, Photoroyalty 30, polya_olya 31, Richard Peterson 31, 34, 35, 71, Roman Sigaev 47, 50, 51, 73, Roman Silantev 28, 34, 35, 71, Romrodphoto 6, Ronald Sumners 44, 50, 51, 73, RTimages 28, 34, 71, Ruth Black 52, 58, 59, 74, Soumen Tarafder 66, spass 30, Suradech Prapairat 18, Syda Productions 62, uzhursky 14, VGstockstudio 22, VIS Fine Art 23, 26, 51, 70, Vladvm 15, 18, 69, Volosina 60, 75, wavebreakmedia 62, Worraket 55, 58, 59, 74, Yellow Cat 15, 18, 69

Illustrated by Tamara Joubert (unit openers and stories) and Christos Skaltsas (Hyphen)

Cover Image: Rafa & Nathalie Studio

Unit 1

Page 4

Page 7

Unit 2

Page 12

Page 14

Unit 3

Page 20

Page 23

Unit 4

Page 28

Page 31

Unit 5

Page 36

Page 39

   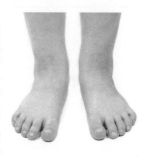

Unit 6

Page 44

Page 47

Unit 7

Page 52

Page 55

Unit 8

Page 60

Page 63